Norwich Sketches

by David Poole of Norwich

Acknowledgements
I am very grateful to Alan Atherton the librarian, Eastern Counties Newspapers for allowing access to the photographic files and loaning me several very fine photographs, especially the view of St. Giles and St. John's taken from the fire station in Bethel Street.
Clifford Temple, a well known local historian, produced a mass of visual evidence in the form of his private photographic collection, from which he swopped me the memorable shot of the bowler-hatted newsboy (Billy) on page 51 in exchange for a copy of my last book, Norfolk Coast Sketches
I am especially grateful to the many people who kindly allowed me to include within this third sketch book their paintings which I have captioned as clearly as possible in the text.

First published May 1981

Hardback edition ISBN 0 9506592 3 1
Paperback edition ISBN 0 9506592 2 3

Repro by Photomation, Norwich
Printed and bound in the United Kingdom by Page Bros (Norwich) Ltd.

Foreword

What does Norwich mean to me, as a dwellingplace what has it done to endear itself within my consciousness?

I first experienced its atmosphere when I used it as a place of enjoyment whilst being stationed at relatively nearby R.A.F. Watton during the years 1958 - 1963. They were indifferent years filled with a great deal of self-indulgence but towards the end of the period I was awakened from my slothfulness artistically by a young woman who at the time was attending Norwich. The sight of her handiwork triggered off my own lapsed love of artistic creativity and so I began clumsily but determinedly to try drawing again.

It is difficult to assess relative influences for all of us whether we are aware or not, are being influenced by our environment and by the dwellers within it.

How strangely life moves at times, the city that I had barely looked at gave to me my most treasured tangible possession: Jenny my long-suffering wife. The quiet slumbering city wove its strands tighter as this spirited daughter stood firm against my many impoverishments.

It seemed sensible enough to try settling down hereabouts back in 1965 as we made the difficult transition from the R.A.F. to civilian life. To the city we brought, not a lot: a relatively penniless little family prepared to make a fresh start, one husband searching for a job as a trainee artist, one wife fortunately able to find work as an State Registered Nurse on nights at St. Helens. one son Simon almost two years old. The city took our son three and a half years later but brought to us two delightful daughters full of life and stimulus.

Within the city I found tremendous visual stimulus and training especially commercially: print-wise and architectural-wise at the long-established excellent training ground of Jarrold & Sons.

Now my eyes were rising up from surveying my feet and the greyness of the pavements, and stimulated by the oftentimes exquisite beauty of the print I saw in the Jarrold's factory; forced also to submerge myself in an agony of artistic perfection-seeking to soak up the awful tragedy of our son's dying, I pressed on .... daring to exhibit my impoverished and often crude work.

Then this city showed me its patient kindness in so many other ways: in the H.J. Sexton Norwich Arts Trust:- the lovely Assembly Rooms as a place to exhibit my work annually; it brought me its kindness in and through the local press and to reporters such as Frank Gordon and Neville Miller I shall be long indebted for their encouragement of my draughtsmanship and finally in this respect to many people who have 'patronised' me purchasing a drawing or painting: particularly I am grateful to our friends Rod and Moira Spokes, for their encouragement.

Remembering Alec Cotman reminds of the city's continued spell upon me as it stimulates me through its rich heritage of artistic achievement and continues so to do everytime my being is blessed with its sight.

Page Bros (Norwich) Ltd.

Terry Attwood

Derek Russen

Ron Colman

Russell Miller

Derek Holmes

Albert Bowers

Barbara Calver

John Marrison

Bert Gaul

Page Bros (Norwich) Ltd.

Reg Quantrell

Jean Diggins

Ken Hendry

The years 1980 and 1981 have been hard-hitting towards Britain's manufacturing base as vital and stringent economies have swept away a disturbingly large number of companies and have caused many others to trim down operational bases both in personnel and equipment.
Therefore I am doubly grateful that these two Norwich-based firms are surviving.
My deep gratitude is extended to all the staff of both firms from whose number sixteen have been drawn as representative of the outstanding skill, patience, guidance and high quality of manufacture with which I have been faithfully served.

Paul Waller

Photomation Graphic Arts

Mike Tetlow

Steve Foster

Paul Foster

12 James and Ann Tillett 12
James and Ann Tillett

FLIXTON & STUART
ROOMS are AVAILABLE for
PRIVATE HIRE during
EVERY NIGHT of the week

THE MONASTERY
ELM HILL CRAFT SHOP

BRITONS ARMS
COFFEE
HOUSE
CLOSED ON SUNDAYS
CLOSED

25

opposite page : The Stamp Shop, Elm Hill.

It really is remarkable that this beautiful street was saved by one vote at a Council meeting to consider its entire demolition. Now of course it is hard to imagine what the area looked like when the demolition proposal hung over it like a pall: certainly there would have been little sparkle about the place; mainly neglect and an air of depression.
The transformation has not taken place in a matter of a months but has been a gradual refining process over several years.
As a shopping centre it can give the impression of being exclusive but with patient observation there are awaiting to be 'discovered' very reasonable shops and services as well as the expensive ones such as Mandells Gallery wherein we have seen the work of some local artists such as Stephen Batchelder 1849-1932 skyrocket in price because of the increased popularity of his watercolours and the very astute presentation of them by Geoffrey Allen. Yet even in Mandells you can occasionally find a 'bargain'. A few years ago I bought a watercolour sketch of a country lane by A. J. Stark and a similar work of Blakeney by Gerald Ackermann R.I. Each cost me about fifty pounds. Jenny and I drew a great deal of pleasure from these gentle works and for me especially they were instructive to my own strivings as an artist.
Another fascinating shop at the foot of Elm Hill is Studio 69 on the corner and also the Framemakers and Gallery a little further up the street. Like Elizabeth Watson's Craft Shop, illustrated on left of pages 8 and 9, the shop and gallery are like Aladdin's caves, and the service I have always found to be most cheerful and well-mannered, whether I am buying a postcard or arranging the framing of seventy five original drawings.
Though sadly some very unwelcome visitors settled in the old tree and proceeded to give it a fatal dose of Dutch Elm fungus and the glorious tree had to be sawn down, now we have, I think its a London Plane, guaranteed to grow very quickly to a splendid height.
Charisma is another giftshop, run by Christians endeavouring especially to encourage brothers and sisters in the Lord to market their work. I bought Jenny a most healthy looking Leopard Lily potted plant and then was lumbered with the very awkward job of helping Mr. Powley from Foulsham carry his large delivery of office furniture via the tiny winding staircase to the first floor.
So this gem of a street grows on and incidentally may the Council hear sympathetically, the views of the traders who want cars to continue to bring it 'normal trading life'.

see pages 6 and 7 : The Tourist Information Centre in the 15th-century Augustine Steward's House in Tombland and opposite the Erpingham Gateway to the cathedral.

see pages 8 and 9 : Looking past the Britons Arms, once a public house now a most friendly restaurant, and down the enchanting cobbled street known as Elm Hill.

Elm Hill in Summertime.

A party of schoolchildren descend or more accurately, begin to ascend the hill accompanied by their teacher. It is interesting to note that I am writing up these notes or captions in March 1981 a little less than a year after I watched this incident. Now outside the rain is pouring steadily down upon a very wet earth but then, last year the small schoolparty were bathed in generous sunshine that made the world seem so very beautifully right — ah! sadly like the sunlight that is such an elusive truth. Yet on that lovely day the sun penetrated deep into the hard shining cobbles and warmed the world putting a sparkle into it. At the head of the schoolparty outside his 'Little Gallery' stands Ivor Hook the art dealer who has surely seen some beautiful work in his time but on this particular day was content to stand outside his gallery and enjoy the unsurpassable beauty of life thriving outside his dimmed by comparison collection of paintings. For an artist struggles to capture a moment in time and yet Ivor in perhaps several minutes saw enough incident and beauty to fill a thousand galleries.

Whatever form the creativity takes: art — drawing, painting or sculpture; music or writing ... it surely can only be fragmentary. But for all that the sight or sound; the awareness of something movingly meaningful from the hand of a fellow human being is northeless wonderful. Such is artistic stimulus: from the earliest brilliant though crude cave paintings to the classic mountaintops of artistic achievements through to today's mixture of revivalism on the one hand and almost abject despairing spiritual emptiness on the other.

I am beginning to understand perhaps too slowly and grudgingly that such emptiness is the power of artistic expression triumphing yet again. Irrepressibly it seems man reveals his deepest needs this way, surprisingly indifferent to ridicule;

and so down the years we have record of man struggling to communicate spiritually. I dont particularly like to see an empty canvas; a slashed canvas; a geometric pattern in place of the wonders of natural form but these so lucidly cry out the hopelessness and emptiness felt by many living in this age of Nuclear nastiness. Praise God that he pours out His light impartially, generously upon us all.

overleaf pages 14 and 15
'Tombland looking towards the Maid's Head Hotel,' in the possession of Mr. & Mrs. Ron Bobbins.

David Poole

To enter more thoroughly into the ancient character of the city it is useful to study such excellent books as "Old Norwich A Collection of Paintings, Prints and Drawings of an Ancient City" by Alec Cotman and Francis Hawcroft.

Whilst Norwich is yet endowed with some rich treasury of ancient architecture it has, on the other hand, suffered some irretrievable losses. Amongst these and salient stand the wall-gates: the fortified entrances into the old city. Amongst these were St. Stephen's or Nedeham Gate. Queen Elizabeth I rode on horseback through this gateway when she visited the city in 1578.

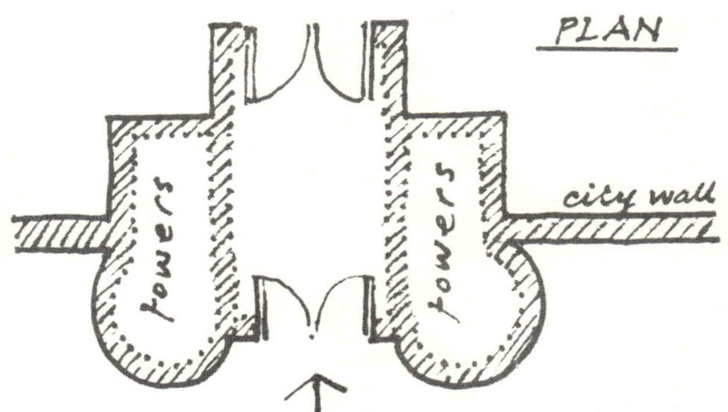

St. Stephen's Gate
(outside)

The walls and gates were constructed at the start in 1294 and not finished until 48 years later in 1342.

In 1790 the Bishop Gate which had been constructed on the city end of Bishop's Bridge had fallen into bad repair and was subsequently demolished. St. Stephen's was pulled down in 1793, Ber Street in 1807 and Magdalen Gate in 1808. The change in warfare techniques brought about the decline and hastened the disinterest in what we regard as memorable but to the transporter of the day were simply objectionable obstacles to his freer passage into and out of the city. So all the gates came down. Thus the cathedral gates, especially the Ethelbert in the corner of Tombland and The Bishop's Palace Gate and the third surviving gate The Erpingham opposite the West end of the cathedral are precious indeed in showing us the scale and character of these lost Medieval gates which once encircled the city complete with a fairly business-like defensive wall; remnants of the wall can still be seen, the most impressive section being that on Carrow Hill and the singular finest unit being Cow Tower – a thick walled brute of structure, virtually a round castle keep squatting like a giant where the River Wensum bends sharply near Kett's Hill. Kett and his rebels attacked the fortified city in 1549 and they fought their way into the heart of it through the Bridge Gate eventually capturing the mayor and holding him hostage. But the brief rebellion ended disasterously with Kett hung from the Castle walls.

The Bishop's Palace Gateway   in the possession of Dr. & Mrs. David Varvel.

Do you remember the years just after the Second World War? Ah yes! many of you are far too young; well anyway I was just past the age of nine. We train spotted, (they were really worth seeing then in all their steamy muck and brassy glory) car spotted and got pretty spotty with things like chicken pox but the aspect I remember was the drabness of much of our materials: all the cars were black — that is those few cars that we gazed at in an expansive almost empty showroom or recorded registration numbers of cars that glided by luxuriously to and from Manchester. I went to a grammar school in my home town of Sale which insisted on uniform: black blazer, grey rings about the cuffs, grey flannel shorts and eventually trousers, black cap and shoes. It was very smart shortly after leaving the shop but subjected relentlessly to the ignoble, inconsiderate treatment of being means tested on playgrounds, playing fields, the bark of trees, harsh treatment with cane, used as goalmarkers, temporary pillows etc it soon became less than smart and particularly raggy, baggy and saggy.

I get a great deal of pleasure these days from seeing the liberated fashions churned out by the Rag Trade whilst seeing in much evidence the stubborn, conservative and sober style of apparel still surviving three decades on: but it would be difficult to match the elementary smart contrast of black and white with a few shades of grey thrown in for a little variety.

Yes the city benefits from the rich range of dress commonly seen about the streets.

I become sometimes almost mesmerised at the variety of dress I see, at the sheer attractiveness of an ever-moving sea of people all uniquely different. And when I see in the Close or on Earlham Road on a Sunday morning parties of schoolchildren identically uniformed it stirs sometimes a gentle rememberance of those often blissful days just after the war when a number of unfortunate teachers strove to break through my daydreaming.

The Cathedral from the South and Inner Close.

I recall seeing a tall thin bald-headed verger or canon dressed in a flowing black vestment that skirted the ground and was belted at the waist. He was hatless and being pulled vigourously along by two beautiful tallish dogs. Such could have been an incident half a century ago. This is part of the fascination of the Cathedral Close its relative timelessness, its very ancient beauty, its extraordinary peace within the heart of the city.

9
8

on the opposite page: 'Bishop's Bridge'. It really does look Medieval and one interesting point is that the merry mischieviousness of the stonemason's' could not resist carving faces deep inside the arches – not gargoyles but stone signatures of satisfaction at a job thoroughly well done. The bridge remember, was a vital accessway most probably for the cathedral community giving access to the extensive grazing afforded by Mousehold Heath. The defensive gateway with its four slim octagonal towers had been pulled down in 1790. Today the bridge carries the full quota of modern traffic save the juggernauts and despite this keeps at moments of quiet a magical atmosphere.

below: 'The Erpingham Gateway' from a watercolour drawing kindly loaned by Miss E. Burrows.
On the narrow plot of land behind the as yet red letter box once stood Dr. Cooper's house, a most lovely property shouldering against the gate and whose roof was just about half a metre short of the peak above the gate.

This is one of my favourite views of the cathedral, standing viewing the East end with its graceful flying buttresses and statued pediments; and the cathedral rising up so gracefully with its magnificent spire pointing heavenwards dwarfing we little people below who are so inclined to look downward and not upward to God when we are in daily need.

The Erpingham Gate from Dr. Cooper's lawn. The seated statues right at the top of the flanking pillars have become so smoothed by erosion that they look as though they were carved by Henry Moore.
The gateway was erected by Sir Thomas Erpingham, who fought at Agincourt. A kneeling statue of Sir Thomas fills the niche above the archway. The gateway, built about 1420, faces the West front of the Cathedral.

overleaf : Houses in the Lower Close, fairly near Pull's Ferry.

27

Looking back to the previous two pages 24 and 25, 'Houses in the Lower Close', brings back a wave of happy memories. Several of the drawings in this book were executed on the spot. Relatively early in the morning I would cycle down into the city whizzing down Kett's or St. James' Hill, my eyes streaming, my mind mumbling and muttering about brakes and dignity and my heart singing for joy at the effortless freedom of it and the beauty that lay before me. Always when I take the hill descents into the city I am rewarded by the wonder of such a place nestled against Mousehold like a cat in a basket. With relief I free-wheel to Bishop's Bridge and cross the Wensum passing into Bishopgate and by the Red Lion. Pedalling past the home of the late Leslie Davenport a great inspiration to any would-be city artist. He could be seen working outside in pretty near all weathers scrubbing away at one of his vigourous chalk drawings. Soon into Palace Plain after passing The Great Hospital and St. Helen's House then The Adam and Eve public house. Then through the Ethelbert Gate into The Close and coming alongside the houses to be drawn I would lean my bicycle against a wall and set up my easel which had survived the rigourous ride. Because of the length of time I expected to spend on the spot, I had a folding stool, very low but very appreciated. With a preliminary key sketch, to give me help in composition, scale and so on, accomplished; I pressed on to the full-size drawing. The light was marvellous: in the mornings I was shadowed by the wall and throughout the days I felt it wise to wear sun glasses because the white and pastel-painted houses were glaring strongly in the sunlight.

From the little house in the centre of the drawing, an interesting gentle drama ensued. Over the three days I spent on the spot I was entertained and delighted to witness something of the birth of a baby. It was the sight of the grandmother the day mother and baby came home from hospital that was most compelling. Grandmother must have walked into the road and peered anxiously up towards Ethelbert Gate four or five times. She epitomised the loving grandparent unable to sit indoors and to patiently wait for her daughters return. At last the car came with its extra special passenger and late that afternoon the grandmother proudly wheeled out the pram, cooing and caressing but now content as she, enraptured, gazed at this latest precious gift.

I experienced something else during those sixteen hours: times when a great peace descended about the place, when the roaring traffic of the city like a marauding medieval army grew faint and then my ears discovered the gentler sounds of footfalls, children's voices, bells quietly ringing, pigeons calling and cooing .... it was a recuperative, refreshing time for me.

opposite: The Erpingham Gate seen from the Cathedral side, and through the arch can be seen part of The Samson and Hercules building the main dance hall for the city but also having banquet hall facilities.

Part of Norwich School, the School Chapel sited on the Canonry of the Priest's College.

There seems to have been a school connected with the Cathedral since the eleventh century; one of the earliest definite references to the School occurs in 1240. The medieval school was situated near the river in the vicinity of the Great Hospital. No trace of these buildings remains and the school moved to the Great Hospital and later to the church of the Black Friars.

In the company of tourists and office workers I was spending a lunch break in the vicinity of the Upper Close and saw the man above blissfully laid out on the grass. He reminded me of a fleshier version of the type of pious statue that can be seen decorating a bishop's tomb. My daughter Susan has the irritating habit of unconcernedly lying on top of churchyard tombs with her hands clasped on her chest and pointing upwards. It naturally gave me a bit of a chill when she first did it in the churchyard of Harrow on the Hill.

on the right : Dick Condon the extraordinary manager of The Theatre Royal, Norwich who has singularly demonstrated that with a combination of knowledge, courage, will-power, good humour and a seemingly tireless devotion an ailing enterprise can be transformed into what is now recognised as the best provincial theatre.

Mr. Chilvers, watch repairer who can be observed with his colleague, Mr. Dowe at work in their shop at the top of St. Andrew's Hill.

opposite: Tombland Alley one of the few surviving passageways of medieval Norwich. Its entrance from Tombland is through an arch under the fifteenth-century Augustine Steward's House immediately opposite the Erpingham gate of the Cathedral Close.
Tombland Alley is frequently extremely quiet for it is shielded on all sides by substantial tall buildings including the church of St. George's. The alleyway leads into Princes Street after negotiating the base of the aforementioned church tower. Princes Street is narrow and paved with setts of granite that add to its ancient feel but it has become a relatively busy throughfare to Elm Hill and St. Andrew's Plain.
Tombland's importance as a focal point of the city has been increased by the Tourist Industry. There is a tremendous amount to see in Norwich but I think it not unreasonable to say that the most popular area is in the vicinity of the Cathedral: Tombland. Nowadays modern traffic streams through so there is an almost constant roar of engines, through the full range of traffic. Just occasionally with tantalising stimulus the noise disappears and for a brief interlude the area resumes its ancient feel as not a car, motorbike or bus destroys the peace. Film-makers have employed it for it offers a beautiful backdrop with its unrivalled range of architecture with lime, plane and birch trees softening and sweetening the acrid air.
It was the 'Civic Square' of Saxon

Norwich. Here once stood The Earl's palace and before that the lodge of the East Anglian Kings together with St. Michael's Church and other buildings necessary to Anglo-Saxon government. The Saxons founded English democracy and here in Tombland must have struggled to construct its principles; they also

used it as a Market Place, but the Normans rather than adapting it for their own purposes confiscated it and gave it to the Cathedral monks, yet gradually the Norwich citizens regained control of this highly regarded area.
Today it survives as an open space bordered by some brilliant examples of medieval, Tudor and Georgian architecture. It is indisputably one of the most interesting parts of the city perhaps especially in the summer months when it is teeming with tourists from all over the world. As the city becomes more widely known this trend will continue for there is nowhere else quite like Tombland.

As Tombland terminates at its northern end the road forks to pass on one side of The Maid's Hotel into Wensum Street and on the other into Palace Street. I believe the illustration above shows the mock-Tudoring constructed this century to the hotel, although the hotel has sections which date back to much earlier times when it was a much regarded coaching inn.

The Louis Marchesi public house and The Black Horse Bookshop provide

a balancing interest on the opposite side of Wensum Street.
The statue of Edith Cavell occupies a hazardous position in front of the hotel – but reminding us of the risks this martyr took to help British Troops towards freedom in the First World War.

Daphne Gosden who with her husband runs the Stationery Shop in Queen's Street. Much to my surprise Daphne was one of several shopkeepers or booksellers who gave me warm encouragement on the publishing of the previous two sketchbooks: Broadland Sketches and Norfolk Coast Sketches.

As you can see the sketch below was in many ways a brief exercise and the one opposite of Tombland, from a first floor window looking towards St. George's was only a shade less brief but captures a little of the pedestrian activity one wet afternoon. Three stalls and a kiosk once stood near the trees but these were eventually removed after the council lost a High Court case brought by a citizen in order to defend Tombland as a permanent open space.

Palace Street, Norwich.
Preliminary sketch for
Norwich Sketches 1979

Repairing the tower of St. Michael at Plea.

opposite page: The tower of St. Michael at Plea under repair.
above: a rapidly drawn sketch of part of the Haymarket.
at left: Abdullah Job at my drawing class in Wensum Lodge.
Norwich has experienced considerable change since the forties and there has been an influx of we "foreigners" into this once very quiet backwater of England. I believe this quieter invasion has been very stimulating to the city's life as unique characters from Guernsey, Ireland, the Far East and Africa and elsewhere impart their own colour into the tapestry of the place.

RAF
CAREERS
INFORMATION

opposite : Bridewell Alley which runs down in narrow paved passage from Bedford Street to St. Andrews Street but also runs by the church and museum to connect with St. Andrew's Hill. The Alley derives its name from the house built in about 1370 by the father of William Appleyard (first Mayor of Norwich), which building subsequently was made a Bridewell (prison) in 1583. Today it is a four-sided building enclosing a small quadrangular paved garden or court; its interior rooms have been employed as a museum of trades and local industry and commerce. There are some splendid exhibits from peacefully plodding pendulum clocks to various forms of roof covering: tile, thatch and the like; a blacksmith's shop even to the smouldering fire and then looms reminding us of the vigourous and prosperous weaving industry that thrived in Norwich and about the surrounding county singularly marked to us in this present age by the unique collection of medieval churches that stand sentinel to such times. There are some interesting guild signs and signboards, carts and agricultural and fishery tools and equipment on exhibition. The Curator, David Jones is keen to help any genuine enquirers or researchers as too are the staff. Turning to the outside again there is a plaque which proudly acclaims the wall opposite St. Andrew's church to be finest piece of flintwork in England.
Bridewell is a wonderful way containing fascinating shops like Hovells principally trading in basketwork but displays a good deal of pine furniture; The Mustard Shop: shop window to the large local firm of Reckitt and Colmans; tailors, bakers, antique shop, newsagents, hairdressers, angling, cafe and so on — a short, narrow but fascinating treat of a street.

below: John Hornagold and Dick Futter hand bookbinders working at George Garnham's in Pottergate. Their workshop is a wonderful place lit with arched weaver's windows that may be conducive to fine natural light but can be very cold, around the walls are shelves of books and papers, racks of wheeled foil-blocking tools and then there is the complicated machine ruler, like something out of the nineteenth century.

Bernard Dorman and his daughter, Catherine, who with Mrs. Dorman comprise a clear example of many of the fine family businesses in the city. Bernard recently aquired the adjacent car showroom and has converted it into a galleried extension to his Blackhorse Bookshop. giving the bookshop a sort of library browsiness especially on the gallery and in quieter periods.

London Street like a magnet, draws various 'outreachers' such as at Christmas-time the sight and stirring sound of a small group of musicians from The Salvation Army which has its Citadel in Ber Street; then I've seen on several occasions of late, a very tall busker or street musician who against the deep chill of the wintered stone and brick of the street and its buildings, wears a long black overcoat and wool hat from out of which literally flows his lengthy gingerish-coloured hair. He has large rather staring yet appealing eyes and as with many street musicians, he plays his guitar passably well. I saw him again a week or so ago in the Bridewell Alley cafe where many 'characters' congregate behind the large picture window looking out into the alley over cups of tea and through clouds of smoke. I thought, 'What a wonderful drawing he would make!' And lately I often react to such a person in this way and gently regret that I cannot break off what I am doing and set about some sketches of an interesting head. Yet the discipline of keeping hands on the plough and not looking back is important in order to complete a relatively straight furrow. I believe as yet, I've a good way to go before I have learned this discipline more thoroughly – for I know just how much time is lost through meandering inclinations taking me away from a determined. On the other hand, occasional inspired diversions are invaluable to keeping a better sense of experimentation and development. One of these days I must take my sketch pad into the cafe.

above: London Street, thanks to probably Continental plaza-type influence the Council took the plunge and shut off the traffic. Just as now with regard to the proposed closure to traffic of Gentleman's Walk, there were fears that trade would be killed off, but the result has been startlingly the reverse and the once dangerous street is now filled with a flood of shoppers at ease in its calm atmosphere.

Jarrolds Department Store seen from the corner flower stall of The Market, showing something of the graciously designed pillared and decorated part of the store. Further to the right of this sketch into London Street is perhaps the most interesting architectural feature of any part of the building's exterior and that is the slim section of deep red decorated brickwork designed by Edward Skipper and utilising a great deal of moulded brickwork in some very detailed panels.

Sketched below is Barbara Gaskin the buyer for the book department and on the right below, Anita Ward section buyer. It is hard to put into words the appreciation I have towards these encouraging buyers and their colleagues who, though at times under considerable pressure, remain polite and clear-minded.

The Assembly House. I first approached its imposing entrance in 1969 and I recall almost turning around and walking away because I felt so out of keeping with such an imposing place. But I walked on and entered its splendid interior and enjoyed and shall continue to delight in its balanced, stately beauty so skilfully designed into this treasuresome gift from H. J. Sexton to the city. So please do not let yourselves be put off by the 'posh'-looking exterior but go in and enjoy the place: have a pot of tea and a scrumptious cake in the restaurant wherein has dined the charming Queen Mother and other notables. There are exhibitions to see, concerts in the marvellous Music Room, the Noverre Cinema and other interesting aspects.

at left: Russell Watering a long-standing much-loved member of the staff.

A drawing of The Market with the Sir Garnet Wolsley public house and St. Peter Mancroft's and other buildings overshadowing but far from overpowering the teeming tantalising trading square in the centre of the city resplendent with its rows of striped canvas roofed stalls, beaming brightly, always cheerful with flowers, fruit and gleaming fish, full of life, conversation and cheery, chatty trade and cameraderie about the stalls.

DUNN & Co
DUNN & Co
DUNN
NDS

see previous two pages 48 and 49
London Street, looking towards the Guildhall and the clocktower of the controversial City Hall building of which J. Wentworth-Day wrote back in the fifties: "Despite the outburst of muddled materialism in the 1930's, which resulted in the destruction of ancient beauty and the erection of the City Hall – each time I look at it I expect to hear railway wagons being shunted in its unlovely interior."
An extremely harsh view but it is easy to forget the 'immediate' impact a new building can have upon one's senses. In the last ten years whilst spending much of that time endeavouring to provide a building design – architectural service, I have slowly realised that it is sometimes necessary to carefully allot to a new building the benefit of the benevolent brush of time which has the beautifying effect of softening hard lines and clean new material colours until somewhat magically, the 'eyesore' softens and nestles in amongst its neighbours.

In the reign of Henry VIII on the dissolution of the monasteries all too many already powerful men seized common lands which were the rightful property of the village poor. These now hard-pressed peasants gathered together under a leader called Kett, a man of some education and upright principles; and marched through Norwich to Mousehold Heath. Twenty thousand men camped in turf huts roofed with boughs and from this determined company a petition was sent to the King pleading their cause, it read: "rede-grounde and meadowe grounde may be at suche price as they were in the first yere of King henry the seventh; that all bushells within your realm be of one stice, that is to say, to be in measure eight gallons; that prests or vicars that be not able to preche and sett forthe the woorde of God to hys parisheners may be thereby putt from hys benyfice; that all bonde men may be ffre, for God made all ffre with hys precious bloode sheddyng (Jesus died to set all of us, who accept him as Lord, free of every bondage); that all ryvers may be ffre and common to all men for fyshyng and passage; that the pore mariners or fyshermene may have whole profights of their fyshyngs as purpses (porpoises), grampes (grampuses), whalles, or any grett fyshe, so it be not prejudicall to your grace;" that in every parish someone might be appointed to, "teche pore mens chyldren of ther parysshe the boke called the Cathakysme and the prymer."

to the right: Mr. Heard the late and colourful newsboy who together with his much smaller colleague at the far left made a charming partnership. The smaller newsboy is still to be seen.

Incredibly, neither King, Privy Council or Parliament could establish a reasonable compromise rather than giving into the blunt instrument of bloodshed. Kett and his company refused the King's offer of pardon for they saw themselves not as wicked men but as innocent and just men. The battles commenced and the Norfolkmen fought with a fierce fury overwhelming the Marquis of Northampton's force. But the second force under the Earl of Warwick included many foreign mercenaries who eventually overwhelmed the rebels fighting through the city and finally against a last stand on Mousehold Heath. Kett was hanged from the walls of the Norman Keep; nine of his principal lieutenants were hung from the oak of reformation and forty five more rebels were hung, drawn and quartered in Norwich Market Place.

above : Market stalls temporarily positioned by St. Peter Mancroft's from a watercolour sketch loaned by Dr. Iris Ashkin.

To see the stalls scattered about the upper streets of Bethel and St. Giles made a refreshing change during the laying on of piped water, electricity and proper paving to the market site. Many people groaned when they saw the regimented stalls being constructed for one of attractive features of such a place had been the contrast from the more orderly and permanent shops surrounding the site. Fortunately the inevitable modifications have been added to the stalls by the traders that begin to break down the too-arranged appearance; the canvas roofs have faded and the place begins to recover something of its old casual air whilst having gained the benefit of covered ways between the rows of stalls which enhance the weather protection as too do the newly constructed market stalls.

above : The Flower Stall corner of the market from an oil sketch kindly loaned by Mr. & Mrs. E.G. Adams.

previous two pages 52 and 53 : A hazy sunny afternoon by the market. Kindly loaned by Mrs. Beryl Kett.

The wise moving of the Cattle Market from the Castle site to Harford Bridges inevitably robbed the city of an ancient charm but of course it was no longer sensible to drive cattle, sheep, pigs and other creatures indifferent to the Highway Code through a busy city however picturesque it appeared, but there still remains a ruralistic feel to the place — though at times when planners put traffic lights on roundabouts and mess up their sequence the patience of even a normally peaceful rustic is sorely tried.

W.R. BULLEN
29 Goldsmith W.R. BULLEN LTD Silversmiths
SWAN LANE

Boots

St. Stephen's Church in Rampant Horse Street, a relatively careful drawing of about sixteen hours from a position sheltered beneath Debenham's canopy just within Brigg Street. Interestingly, it was a few yards up Brigg Street into The Haymarket that I began to 'ease' myself into the difficultly of drawing live in the city by first trying a rapid sketch of Snob and beyond illustrated in the earlier part of this book. Drawing the church was reasonably alright because my easel was set up hard against the store's display windows and I was consequently out of the main stream of pedestrian traffic. But in the cases of the two previous double page spreads — especially the drawing of London Street on pages 56 and 57, I found it very hard to remain calm and very nearly became agitated when a party of foreign youths gathered closely around my easel and one of them inevitably carelessly caught one its legs with his foot. But fortunately it cooled down and I was able to complete the drawing in spite of the lunchtime flood of foot-powered folk spilling out of factories, offices and shops for a breath of relatively fresh air.

The graffitied tree is symptomatic of some of the youths — sadly many of whom are unemployed and disenchanted; some of whom felt I was fair sport for their mob mischief until they learned that I was prepared to protect the right to work unmolested.

{see previous pages 56 and 57
{London Street in Summer of 1980.

{see previous pages 58 and 59
{Gentleman's Walk from Hayhill.

St Stephen's

E. BAYLISS
WRIGHT & Co
Drawing & Office
Equipment

Prince of Wales Road, looking towards the Royal Hotel, another Edward Skipper building and one which has recently escaped being demolished only by the strongest of protests from the conservationists. The Hotel would be sorely missed as it is quite unique with its kind of French chateau - like appearance. It looked eerie and wonderful one early Winter's evening silhouetted against a stormy yet brilliantly lit moonlit sky.

Part of St. Giles with but a hint of its rich architecture, much Georgian but some interesting stone-fronted buildings that I have determined one day to make a closer study of. For this little sketch I took refuge in the nearby churchyard of St. Giles and peered past the railings down the street, surprising passers-by who caught sight of me squatting like an exhibit at a zoo, nontheless I enjoyed the spot under the huge church.

The Church of St. John Timberhill girt around with cooling, beautifying trees.

Traffic roars often noisily impatient and precariously forks as it speeds from Golden Ball Street into Ber Street past Mace the fishmongers or to the right into the short stretch of All Saints St. This sketch was pencilled from Bonds Store from the raised pavement area.

overleaf: Norwich Castle Museum magnificently set upon the ancient and mysterious Early Saxon mound at the heart of the city, encircled partly by Castle Meadow and with ancient elms, oaks and rich emerald grass studded generously with golden daffodils that shout Spring has won.

BELL

The Bell Hotel from Red Lion Street. An oil sketch kindly loaned by Mrs. Claxton.

The illustration below recalls the abuse I received early one Autumn evening last year as I stood drawing, not an imaginary railway scene, but the intricate, gleaming and grimy haunting beauty that was stretched in front me from my vantage point on the railway bridge near Clarence Road and Carrow Road. I was well on with the work using a large sheet of stiff card and then a minibus came along the road and with a yell a youthful lout leaned out of the window and threw the dregs of his beaker of tea or coffee over my drawing. Fortunately I was able to absorb the worst of it with my handkerchief but it had unnerved me so that not surprisingly, I failed to do a good job of it and 'lost it'. More importantly it reminds me of all the protection I have received both on that occasion and on many others when I was vulnerably placed and an interesting target for abuse.

Yes, praise the Lord that he upholds his many promises to us and surrounds us with his powerful protection when we call on him to help us.

If it sounds strange : then taste, test, try the Lord God in Jesus for yourselves... for how can you know the pleasure of something if you haven't the courage to submit to a simple act of faith.

My life, my marriage, my children are being blessed because the Lord indeed is good and the most generous giver of all.

below : a watercolour 'Thorpe Station Approaches' owned by Mr. & Mrs R. Spokes.

overleaf : an oil sketch, 'Chapelfield Gardens', owned by Mrs. Claxton.

GARAGE
HIRE
SERVICE
SERVICE
SELF MOTORING

HERBERT
DUNCAN

GAME
SANDFORDS
GHK 404H
David Poole

Upper St. Giles looking towards St. John's. An oil sketch in the possession of Mr & Mrs Colin Wright.

At first glance the illustration on pages 72 and 73 appears to be an accurate upto date one but in fact a number of the buildings have been swept away for the road system's benefit .... probably a reasonable act but our city is constantly embattled in this way as the following verses attempted to exemplify in June 1973 :— published in the E.E.N.

More than gates have fallen down
within this ancient market town;
Its character taken by the throat
pollutes the air with dust and smoke;
As careless greed and power contrive
to sweep traditional beauty aside.

Build, build, reach up into the air
empty office blocks – oh have a care!
Rusty rods and chips and stones
powdered glue and broken bones;
Grinning teeth and sunburnt backs
careless words and stacks and stacks

Of gentle mellow Norfolk Reds,
like weathered faces – what dread
To see the smallest building crashing down
knowing it once graced this town
Replace, replace – scurry on, hurry on,
like a battle once on can't stop, wont stop

Take a breath, where's your love, your pride
is it all caught up in an easy ride?
Now I'm old, too old to care, to dare
to shout, to raise my feeble voice
My flesh like rubble has fallen down
is cursed, falters and falls to the ground.

One last look at what I leave:
the little place crushed between,
Sky-rising shops and office blocks;
dwellers too preoccupied to care
And when they pause to stand and stare
with hearts unmoved and cold as stone.

see previous pages 72 and 73, A lofty view of St. Giles and St. John's.

Above: from a pen and ink drawing of Peter Crowe's bookshop which can be seen in the middle of the illustration of pages 72 and 73 with the name Herbert Duncan vaguely discernible on the roof. I've purchased from Peter several very helpful books especially on the subject of drawing. His father, Thomas Crowe inspired Peter and has a long-established and fine antiquarian bookshop next door. Beautiful shops they are: quiet and charming full of interest to the bookworms and print collectors. Local books are well worth collecting within of course reasonable means; for few of us can afford the astonishing price of three or four thousand pounds for P.H. Emerson's Victorian photographs.

Norwich over the allotments and Barrack Street from Mousehold Avenue, kindly loaned by Mr & Mrs Chris Kumble.

Unlike both my previous sketchbooks I have observed the city far more frequently and under a wide range of conditions. My own circumstances have changed fairly dramatically ever since my family settled here over fifteen years ago. And with hardly a trace of grudgery I accept that though I should live here a total of forty years or so as Ted Ellis has done, I shall always remain a foreigner. Nontheless the place has gripped me and enchanted me as I have observed its changing character over this significant period. It continues to be a fascinating unfolding account and perhaps the North Eastern viewpoints from Lollard's Pit, Gas Hill, Kett's Hill, the most well known at St James' Hill and my particular favorites as opposite and looking down Silver Road, have the advantage of providing a panoramic view that embraces much of the city and at a glance, give one a sense of grasping immediately just what the city is.

Yet of course it is more than the shells, the exteriors of all the buildings — for its most interesting character is contained in all the marvellous diversity of its inhabitants; an aspect which delights in constant change: has done and seems destined to do so with even more startling rapidity as London overspills — as Chinese and Indian and Greek restauranters and other traders call in their families to share the prosperity they have fairly won. Hundreds of years ago it was case of the absorption of invaders from Italy, Normandy, Scandinavia and refugees from religious persecution such as the Flemish folk who brought their weaving, building and artistic skills to add to the region's intrinsically developed ability. In small measure refugees from Uganda and from amongst the boat-people of Vietnam are the exotic more recent arrivals but in larger numbers it is organisations like H.M.S.O., Bland Payne and to a significant extent the University of East Anglia which are adding width and colour to an already vital population.

below: Mike Walker who has the butchers shop in Upper St. Giles under the trade name, Sandfords.

above: 'The Cathedral from the foot of St. James' Hill. A watercolour in the possession of The Junior School of The Norwich High School for girls .... or should they be described in these sensitive days as young female persons? I prefer girls!

Gurney Court historically interesting as the birthplace of both Harriet Martineau and Elizabeth Fry the famous prison reformer, there are two plaques commemorating these ladies in the arched and panelled entrance passageway that leads off Magdalen Street into the courtyard. John Gurney used this as his original banking house prior to great good fortune enabling him to move his business to Bank Plain and his residence to the beauty of Earlham Hall. The latter hall is now used by the University and the grounds as a public park. As for Gurney Court part has been rented out by the City Council as a residence and the remainder serves as a medical and dental practitioners, each being independant concerns. There is a certain consolation when suffering various agonies in the dental chair, to be reminded of the building's earlier gentler usage and to look through the large semi-circular windows on the first floor dental surgery into the lime trees that soften the pain.

on this double-page spread: an oil sketch of Norwich from the view over the allotments alongside Mousehold Avenue. The painting is in the possession of Rod and Moira Spokes. Although the painting was carried out only towards three years ago, significant changes have taken place: the Steward and Patteson Brewery behind the row of houses have been demolished and new houses with pyramid roofs have been constructed

the allotment end of Cavalry Street that cul de sacs off Barrack Street.
Throughout the seasons, this view point as well as the companion ones around the Mousehold plateau, continues to present the city in a fascinating way; whether its damp and misty and much of the city lies mysteriously obscured with perhaps the cathedral spire floating free suspended in mid air, or during deep winter days when so much detail is again covered by a clean eiderdown of snow and the city gleams: rooftops instead of dark-tiled are shining and sparkling in the gentle light. There are times when ferocious storms charge overhead and the city lies under a patchy pall of angry clouds and brilliant golden skies, this often occuring at sunset. But the sketch below commenced one early morning, was a time when gentle sunlight smiled on her in Autumn.

Studies of Alec Cotman at his home in June 1976

opposite: Unloading Grain by Read's Mill near Carrow Bridge. in the possession of Mrs A. Colls. The port of Norwich has become busier of late, it not being uncommon to see three or four smaller coasters tied up trading in grain, finished metal beams and sections and scrap metal; as well as a variety of smaller craft: spritsail barges, pleasure craft and Broads cruisers.

Alec Cotman: three studies of a very gentle gentleman who I have always found enthusiastic in conversation, cheerful and like his friend Ted Ellis, an absolute mine of information. In fact as I tried to complete the unfinished drawing of Alec at the left, Ted called and the two old friends quickly became absorbed in a file of prints and etchings on Great Yarmouth that Alec possessed and Ted asked to research. One very early print of the river at Yarmouth showed a rowing boat with cabin:

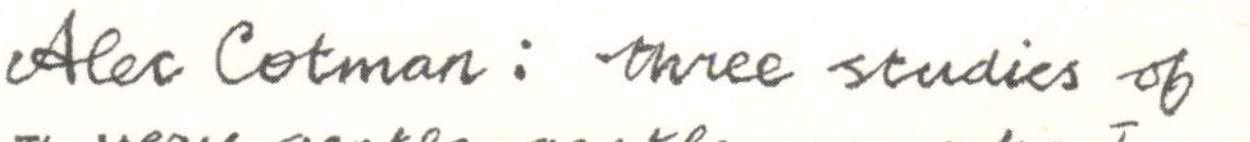

that Ted suggested might have been of the kind that carried Sir Thomas Browne's daughter from Gorleston to Norwich by night, in the late 17 th. Century. Though the sketch remained unfinished I was the richer for seeing these two enthusiastic friends working together.

One benefit of studying a Street map of Norwich is for example, in locating the precise location of the property which carries the handsome Jew's head over a doorway – illustrated on the right; the map can surprise the searcher as in this case: the smiling face shines down on King Street at the junction with Rose Lane and the interesting thing to be learned is the length and importance (especially in past years when the River Wensum carried a great deal of trade out onto the Yare) of King Street. The street runs from Upper King Street, Tombland right down past Carrow Bridge to Bracondale. Nowadays it is perhaps less than of prime importance and yet there is a great deal of business and recreational activity: milling brewing, engineering, food and drinks production, scrap metal

and so on; and on the other hand: tourists are attracted to particularly St. Julien's Alley where Dame Juliana Berners, the fourteenth century mystic and authoress of "Sixteen Revelations of Divine Love was isolated from the world in a small cell – something of which can be seen in the church honouring her name.
On a more practical and contemporary note organisations like The Norwich Lad's Club and the St John's Ambulance Brigade have their homes here as well as the most useful Adult Education Centre, Wensum Lodge.
at left: Ken A. Davis, the warden.

Ken's wife Brenda shares the warden's role and has written the most revealing booklet on "The Story of a House". Unfortunately I cannot convey very much of it herein but Brenda writes: "Jews who lived in the 12th. Century were excluded from all offices of state or positions of authority because their faith denied belief in Christ, they could not become craftsmen or farmers, but they could, and did, use their undoubted abilities in the lending of money for projects great and small. The Church forbade its members to do this but often found itself unable to do without the services so provided, and in Norwich it is probable that Jurnet, the Jew who built this strong stone house, (in .1175 which now is embraced within the more recently constructed Music House, illustrated opposite) also lent the money to finance the building of the great Cathedral.

Jurnet's house with its arched and vaulted cellars was very large for such a time: the internal floor area measured 18'-9" x 52'-6", almost double the size of some Jewish houses in Lincoln. The two rooms separated by a stone wall are now several feet below street level, but were probably at street level in the Middle Ages and used as warehouses and possibly a shop.

Jurnet and his wife Muriel had a son, Isaac and a daughter, Margaret. It was to Isaac that the house and estate passed when Jurnet died; before Michaelmas, in 1197.

Remarkably, it took only a mere 78 years to wrest the house from Jurnet's descendants and for it to be given by Henry III to Lord William de Valeres "for his service". And so on:- Ralf de Erlham, William of Dunwich, 1290 Alan de Frestone, 1316 Sir Constantine de Mortimer, 1368 John de Catfield, Rector of Stratton ... then to the Benhall family and the Felbrigge family passing next to the Yelvertons and in 1488 to Sir John Paston-Knight, (the house remained with the Pastons for nearly 125 years). Through the marriage of Bridget Paston in 1583 the house passed into the Coke family. In 1723 is the first mention of it as a Musick House.

overleaf: Norwich from Silver Road in the possession of Rod and Moira Spokes.

David P

previous double page spread, pages 88 and 89, Bishop's Bridge one beautiful Indian Summertime. An old couple pause whilst crossing the bridge and stand close to where beneath the long demolished Bishopgate rose up and through which Kett's men fought their way into the city. Now only anxious motorists generate antagonism about its vicinity and occasionally it receives a nudge from its dreaming as some hopeless 'admiral' steers amiss and rams the sleeping stone with a Broads cruiser. As the old couple walk on towards the city down Bishopgate, they could glimpse this view below: Norwich Cathedral over a corner of the Norwich School playing fields. Stonemasons could just be seen and they are lightly sketched in, at work repairing the parapet to the East End. The group of houses part of which have the gentle curves of Dutch gabling have been recently renovated. There is a stronger desire these days to preserve our heritage which contrasts very vividly with the indifferent general attitude of earlier "demolition decades".

these pages and pages 92 and 93: Pulls Ferry. The painting on pages 92 and 93 kindly loaned for photographing by Mr. & Mrs. Colin Wright. Just inside the arch can be seen the hinge brackets that carried the ancient watergate, through which wearied bargemen quanted great loads of Caen stone for the building of the Cathedral. This is a view I shall never tire of, so beautiful is its setting.

Psalm 116

I Love the Lord, because he
hath heard my voice and my
supplications.
2. Because he hath inclined his
ear unto me, therefore will I call
upon him as long as I live.
3. The sorrows of death compass-
ed me, and the pains of hell gat
hold upon me: I found trouble
and sorrow.
4. Then called I upon the name
of the Lord; O Lord, I beseech
thee, deliver my soul.
5. Gracious is the Lord, and
righteous; yea our God is
merciful.
6. The Lord preserveth the
simple: I was brought low and he
helped me.
7. Return unto thy rest, O my
soul; for the Lord hath dealt
bountifully with thee.
8. For thou hast delivered my
soul from death, mine eyes from
tears, and my feet from falling.
9. I will walk before the
Lord in the land of the living.
10. I believed, therefore have I
spoken: I was greatly afflicted:
11. I said in my haste, All
men are liars.
12. What shall I render unto
the Lord for all his benefits
toward me?
13. I will take the cup of
salvation, and call upon the
name of the Lord.
14. I will pay my vows unto
the Lord now in the presence
of all his people.
15. Precious in the sight of the
Lord is the death of his
saints.
16. O Lord, truly I am thy
servant; I am thy servant, and
the son of thy handmaid: thou
hast loosed my bonds.
17. I will offer to thee the
sacrifice of thanksgiving, and
will call upon the name of
the Lord.
18. I will pay my vows unto the
Lord now in the presence of
all his people.
19. In the courts of the Lord's
house, in the midst of thee,
O (new) Jerusalem. Praise
ye the Lord.